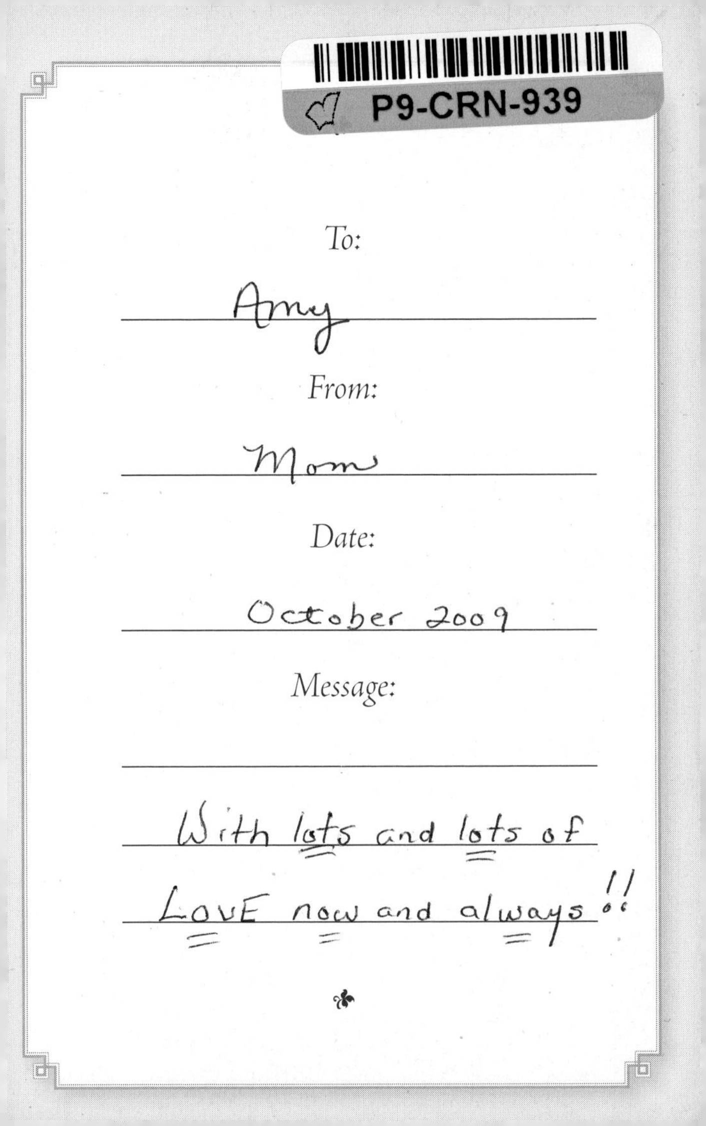

To:

Amy

From:

Mom

Date:

October 2009

Message:

With lots and lots of

LOVE now and always!!

STORMIE OMARTIAN

HARVEST HOUSE PUBLISHERS
EUGENE, OREGON

Cover by Koechel Peterson & Associates, Inc., Minneapolis, Minnesota

Cover photo © piccaya / fotolia

Back cover author photo © Michael Gomez Photography

THE POWER OF PRAYING® THROUGH THE BIBLE BOOK OF PRAYERS

Published by Harvest House Publishers
Eugene, Oregon 97402
www.harvesthousepublishers.com

ISBN-13: 978-0-7369-2533-4

Printed in the United States of America

09 10 11 12 13 14 15 / VP-SK / 12 11 10 9 8 7 6 5 4

Introduction

❧

I have discovered that every verse in the Bible can inspire me to pray in some way. That's why I have included in this book some of the Scriptures I found especially inspirational, along with the prayers I was led to pray as a result of reading them. In my book *The Power of Praying Through the Bible,* I explained specific aspects of each passage that inspired prayer and then I wrote out a short prayer. In this little prayer book, only the specific verses and the prayers are included but not the devotion itself. I did that because having this compact book of prayers handy in your purse, briefcase, glove compartment, backpack, lunch box, or small space near your bedside, workplace, or eating area is very convenient and gives you added opportunities for a quick Bible study and prayer time. Put it someplace where you can seize a few moments out of your busy day to spend time with the Lord in His Word and in prayer.

If you feel led to go deeper into a particular section of Scripture, I recommend looking it up in your Bible and reading the surrounding verses in order to gain a better idea of what that passage is talking about.

I hope these Scriptures and prayers will inspire you to pray every time you read God's Word, and to read God's Word prayerfully. I pray this small book will be a big help to you as you walk ever closer to the Lord.

Stormie Omartian

❧

As the rain and the snow come down from heaven, and do not return to it without watering the earth and making it bud and flourish, so that it yields seed for the sower and bread for the eater, so is my word that goes out from my mouth: It will not return to me empty, but will accomplish what I desire and achieve the purpose for which I sent it.

Isaiah 55:10-11

❧

God's Connection with Us

"The Lord God formed the man from the dust of the ground and breathed into his nostrils the breath of life, and the man became a living being."

Genesis 2:7

❧

Lord, I thank You for the breath of life You have given me. I pray You will breathe new life into me today. Just as You spoke and brought about life in Your magnificent world, help me to speak words that bring life into my own small world as well. How grateful I am to be closely connected to You in every way.

A Walk in the Garden

"Then the man and his wife heard the sound of the Lord God as he was walking in the garden in the cool of the day, and they hid from the Lord God among the trees of the garden. But the Lord God called to the man, 'Where are you?'"

Genesis 3:8-9

❧

Lord, I want more than anything to have a close walk with You. Help me not to forfeit that wonderful intimacy by being drawn toward the distractions of this world. Enable me to hear Your voice calling me so that I will answer without even a moment's delay. Help me to never hide from You for any reason.

Powerful Listening

"Noah was a righteous man, blameless among the people of his time, and he walked with God."

Genesis 6:9

❧

Dear God, help me to live each day with a deep sense of Your presence. I don't want to go through life without taking time to be with You. I want my relationship with You to be so strong that other people recognize Your Spirit in me. Whenever I draw near to You in prayer, help me to hear Your voice speaking to my heart so that I will always follow Your leading.

The Power of God's Promise

"Whenever the rainbow appears in the clouds, I will see it and remember the everlasting covenant between God and all living creatures of every kind on the earth."

Genesis 9:16

❧

Lord, I thank You that You always keep Your promises to me. Help me to understand and remember exactly what Your promises are so that I can recall them in my mind, keep them in my heart, and speak them out loud whenever I need to push doubt away from me. Help me to remember that Jesus is the ultimate proof that You have already kept Your greatest promise to us.

When We Have to Wait

"After this, the word of the Lord came to Abram in a vision: 'Do not be afraid, Abram. I am your shield, your very great reward.' But Abram said, 'O Sovereign Lord, what can you give me since I remain childless and the one who will inherit my estate is Eliezer of Damascus?'"

Genesis 15:1-2

❧

Dear God, help me to have faith enough to believe You will answer my prayers. Give me the patience to wait for the answers to appear. Keep me from giving up and taking matters into my own hands. Instead, enable me to trust that You have heard my prayers and will answer in Your perfect way and time. Help me to rest in peace during times of waiting.

Call on the Name of the Lord

"Isaac built an altar there and called on the name of the LORD. There he pitched his tent, and there his servants dug a well."

GENESIS 26:25

❧

LORD, You are the God of the universe and Lord of my life. I worship You and give glory to Your name. You are holy and wonderful—amazing and awesome—and I thank You for all You have done for me. Because Your Word says You are able to do beyond what I can even think of to ask for, I call on You to meet all of my needs in ways more wonderful than I can even imagine.

The Power of Praise

"Then come, let us go up to Bethel, where I will build an altar to God, who answered me in the day of my distress and who has been with me wherever I have gone."

Genesis 35:3

❧

Almighty God, I worship You for who You are. I thank You for all You have done for me. You have given me power, provision, and purpose. I know I need not fear the future because I see how You have blessed me and protected me in the past. I pray You will always be with me to guide me in the way I should go.

PRAYING FOR YOUR CHILDREN

"He blessed Joseph and said, 'May the God before whom my fathers Abraham and Isaac walked, the God who has been my shepherd all my life to this day, the Angel who has delivered me from all harm—may he bless these boys. May they be called by my name and the names of my fathers Abraham and Isaac, and may they increase greatly upon the earth.'"

GENESIS 48:15-16

❧

HEAVENLY FATHER, teach me to pray for my children and grandchildren and any children You put in my life. Bless each child with a knowledge of who You are and help them to live Your way so they can stay on the path You have for their lives. Enable each child to recognize the gifts and talents You have put in them, and to follow Your leading as they develop and use them for Your glory.

Crying Out to God

"During that long period, the king of Egypt died. The Israelites groaned in their slavery and cried out, and their cry for help because of their slavery went up to God."

Exodus 2:23

❧

Lord, I cry out to You for deliverance from anything that keeps me from becoming all You created me to be. Set me free from everything that separates me from You. Lord, I know that even in the midst of what seems to be the most hopeless situation, You can do Your greatest work. Thank You that You are a God of miracles. I pray You will do a miracle in my life today.

Praying on Behalf of Others

"Pharaoh quickly summoned Moses and Aaron and said, 'I have sinned against the Lord your God and against you. Now forgive my sin once more and pray to the Lord your God to take this deadly plague away from me.'"

Exodus 10:16-17

❧

God, help me to learn to pray in power. Increase my faith to believe for the answers to my prayers. Enable me to become an intercessor for others—especially those who do not know You. I pray that everyone around me will be able to recognize by my life that I am a person of great faith and power in prayer, and that they can trust in the God to whom I pray.

The Power of Little by Little

"Little by little I will drive them out before you, until you have increased enough to take possession of the land."

Exodus 23:30

❧

God, help me to have the patience to wait on You for the answers to my prayers. I confess I want all the answers to appear now, but I know Your timing is perfect. Help me to understand the things that are happening in response to my prayers that I cannot see. Enable me to envision the step-by-step progress that is being made.

WHY WE DO WHAT WE DO

"Aaron's sons Nadab and Abihu took their censers, put fire in them and added incense; and they offered unauthorized fire before the Lord, contrary to his command. So fire came out from the presence of the LORD and consumed them, and they died before the LORD."

LEVITICUS 10:1-2

HOLY FATHER, help me to never be careless about Your ways or Your Word. Enable me to not allow anything that has to do with my worship of You to become lifeless or like ritual that has lost its depth of meaning. Keep the disciplines of prayer, praise, and reading in Your Word fresh and alive in my heart so that I will always have a passionate hunger for Your presence.

Your Day of Atonement

"On this day atonement will be made for you, to cleanse you. Then, before the Lord, you will be clean from all your sins."

Leviticus 16:30

❧

Thank You, Jesus, for paying the price for my sins so that I don't have to. Because of You I have been reconciled to God, and I will never be separated from Him again. Help me to extend to others the love and forgiveness You have given to me. Teach me ways I can show You my gratitude for all You have done.

How Can I Be Holy?

"Speak to the entire assembly of Israel and say to them: 'Be holy because I, the LORD your God, am holy.' "

Leviticus 19:2

❧

DEAR GOD, I worship You for Your greatness and goodness. I praise You for Your holiness. As I worship You, I pray Your holiness will rub off on me. Help me to take on the beauty of Your holiness as I spend time in Your presence. Enable me to become more like You so that Your holiness will make me whole.

The Act of Celebration

"Speak to the Israelites and say to them: 'These are my appointed feasts, the appointed feasts of the Lord, which you are to proclaim as sacred assemblies.'"

Leviticus 23:2

❧

Dear Lord, I celebrate the moment when I came to know You as my Lord. I celebrate the times You have healed me and blessed me. I celebrate Your answers to my prayers and the times You saved me from my own mistakes. I celebrate the wonderful people You have put in my life—especially the ones who have led me to You and taught me to live Your way. I celebrate my life with You.

When You're Feeling Overwhelmed

"I will come down and speak with you there, and I will take of the Spirit that is on you and put the Spirit on them. They will help you carry the burden of the people so that you will not have to carry it alone."

Numbers 11:17

❧

God, I lift up to You the areas of my life that are overwhelming and burdensome. I have not come to You to complain, but rather to seek Your help. Where I have tried to handle everything in my own strength instead of depending on You, I ask Your forgiveness. I pray You will take each burden of my heart and enable me to rise above every challenging situation in my life.

Do Not Be Afraid

"See, the Lord your God has given you the land. Go up and take possession of it as the Lord, the God of your fathers, told you. Do not be afraid; do not be discouraged."

Deuteronomy 1:21

❧

Thank You, Lord, for all the wonderful things You have done for me in the *past,* that You are doing for me *today,* and that You *will* do for me in the *future.* Keep me from fear and discouragement as I look at the challenges ahead. Thank You that You go before me with a plan for battle. I look to You for guidance so I may possess all You have for me.

God Is Near When We Pray

"What other nation is so great as to have their gods near them the way the Lord our God is near us whenever we pray to him?"

Deuteronomy 4:7

❧

Lord, I thank You for being close to me when I pray. Thank You that You hear and will answer me. Thank You that in Your presence there is transformation for my soul and my life. I draw close to You now and ask for an ever-increasing sense of Your presence. I ask that You would help me to pray more and more every day and give me increasing faith to believe for the answers.

Prayers of Intercession

"I feared the anger and wrath of the Lord, for he was angry enough with you to destroy you. But again the Lord listened to me. And the Lord was angry enough with Aaron to destroy him, but at that time I prayed for Aaron too."

Deuteronomy 9:19-20

❧

God, help me to be one of Your faithful and powerful intercessors. Help me to not be so focused on myself and my situation that I don't see how to pray for the needs of others. Give me strong faith to believe that my prayers can make a big difference in their lives. Show me the people I need to pray for today and how I should specifically pray for them.

Looking for God's Will

"Do not let this Book of the Law depart from your mouth; meditate on it day and night, so that you may be careful to do everything written in it. Then you will be prosperous and successful."

Joshua 1:8

❧

Dear Lord, I pray that every time I read Your Word, You will teach me all I need to know. Help me to understand Your truth and speak to me specifically about how each passage I have read relates to my life and to the lives of others. Help me to meditate on Your Word and take steps of obedience so that I can live in Your perfect will and prosper as You have promised.

Confession and Repentance

"But the Israelites said to the Lord, 'We have sinned. Do with us whatever you think best, but please rescue us now.' Then they got rid of the foreign gods among them and served the Lord. And he could bear Israel's misery no longer."

Judges 10:15-16

❧

Dear God, I don't want anything to separate me from You. Nothing is worth that. I want to confess to You anything I have done wrong, and anything not pleasing in Your eyes. Wherever I have worshiped other gods or harbored what You would consider an idol in my life, reveal it to me and I will confess it, repent of it, and get rid of it. I want to serve only You.

Give the Gift of Prayer

"As for me, far be it from me that I should sin against the Lord by failing to pray for you. And I will teach you the way that is good and right."

1 Samuel 12:23

Lord, I pray for each member of my family and for all of my friends and acquaintances to be blessed with peace, good health, provision, and a greater knowledge of You and Your Word. Help me to not be selfish or lazy in my praying. Show me whom else to pray for. May I never sin against You by failing to pray for other people according to Your will.

God Sees Our Heart Toward Him

"Then Saul built an altar to the LORD; it was the first time he had done this."

1 Samuel 14:35

❧

Dear God, I pray I would have a heart of love for You and Your ways that is always pleasing in Your sight. I don't want to be a person who shows love for You with only words. I want to show it with my actions, my obedience to Your laws, and the way I live my life. Thank You that You love me at all times—even when I don't do everything right.

The Quicksand of Temptation

"One evening David got up from his bed and walked around on the roof of the palace. From the roof he saw a woman bathing. The woman was very beautiful, and David sent someone to find out about her."

2 Samuel 11:2-3

❧

Dear God, I pray You will help me to always successfully resist temptation from the moment I am confronted with it. Help me to draw *closer* to You when anything tries to draw me *away* from You. Deliver me from the trap of temptation before I fall into it. Give me the strength, wisdom, and knowledge I need to fully resist temptation at all times.

The Importance of Confession

"David was conscience-stricken after he had counted the fighting men, and he said to the Lord, *'I have sinned greatly in what I have done. Now, O* Lord, *I beg you, take away the guilt of your servant. I have done a very foolish thing.'"*

2 Samuel 24:10

❧

Lord, I pray You would show me any sin in my life so that I can confess it before You. I don't want guilt on my conscience to dilute my walk with You or inhibit my prayers because I am ashamed to come before You in confidence. Help me to always have a repentant heart before You so that I will quickly turn away from sin.

Humbled in His Presence

"Will God really dwell on earth? The heavens, even the highest heaven, cannot contain you. How much less this temple I have built!"

1 Kings 8:27

❧

Dear Lord, I thank You for Your presence in my life. I am thankful and humbled that You—through Your Holy Spirit—live inside me. Help me to never be full of myself, but rather to always be freshly filled with more of You each day. Help me to have a sense of Your presence, especially as I read Your Word and pray and live in obedience to Your ways.

Putting God Above All Else

"As Solomon grew old, his wives turned his heart after other gods, and his heart was not fully devoted to the LORD *his God, as the heart of David his father had been."*

1 Kings 11:4

❧

God, I pray my treasure will always be in You and not in my possessions or the distractions of this world. Help me to never make an idol out of anything or anyone, or put them before You in any way. I give You honor and gratitude for all the good things You have given me. You are my greatest desire, and I put You above all else in my life.

God Will Pour Out as Much as You Can Receive

"Elisha said, 'Go around and ask all your neighbors for empty jars. Don't ask for just a few. Then go inside and shut the door behind you and your sons. Pour oil into all the jars, and as each is filled, put it to one side.'"

2 Kings 4:3-4

❧

Heavenly Father, give me a vision of all You want to do in my life. Help me to not think too small, even when I pray. I want to be available to whatever You have for me and not limit Your blessings by being unprepared to receive them. Enlarge my heart and mind to understand how You can take what I have and expand it beyond what I can imagine.

Open My Eyes, Lord

"Elisha prayed, 'O Lord, open his eyes so he may see.' Then the Lord opened the servant's eyes, and he looked and saw the hills full of horses and chariots of fire all around Elisha. As the enemy came down toward him, Elisha prayed to the Lord, 'Strike these people with blindness.' So he struck them with blindness, as Elisha had asked."

2 Kings 6:17-18

Almighty God, I pray You would open my eyes to see the truth about my situation. Give me clear understanding—especially when I am facing the enemy—of all You are doing in the midst of my situation. Help me to trust Your hand of protection. Enable me to see things from Your perspective so that I can stand strong.

Undeserved Answers to Prayer

"Then Jehoahaz sought the LORD's favor, and the LORD listened to him, for he saw how severely the king of Aram was oppressing Israel. The LORD provided a deliverer for Israel, and they escaped from the power of Aram. So the Israelites lived in their own homes as they had before."

2 Kings 13:4-5

❧

Dear Lord, I thank You that You listen to my prayers and that You answer, not according to my own goodness, but according to Yours. Help me to not let anything discourage me from coming to You in prayer—especially not my own sense that I am undeserving of Your attention and blessing. I come entirely because You are full of grace and mercy.

Be Bold to Ask

"Jabez cried out to the God of Israel, 'Oh, that you would bless me and enlarge my territory! Let your hand be with me, and keep me from harm so that I will be free from pain.' And God granted his request."

1 Chronicles 4:10

❦

God, I thank You for all You have given me. I pray for Your continued blessings, provision, and protection. I pray Your presence will always be with me wherever I go and no matter what happens. Thank You that You are pleased to share Yourself and Your kingdom with me. Enable me to give back to You by helping and blessing others.

PRAY BEFORE YOU ACT

"The Philistines had come and raided the Valley of Rephaim; so David inquired of God: 'Shall I go and attack the Philistines? Will you hand them over to me?' The LORD *answered him, 'Go, I will hand them over to you.'"*

1 CHRONICLES 14:9-10

❦

DEAR LORD, I pray I will always inquire of You first before I take action. I don't want to assume that because You instructed me in a certain way before, You will instruct me in the same way each time I am faced with a similar situation. I don't want to mistakenly think I have all the answers when only You have all the answers for my life.

Inviting God's Pres-ence and Forgiveness

"Now, my God, may your eyes be open and your ears attentive to the prayers offered in this place. Now arise, O Lord God, and come to your resting place, you and the ark of your might. May your priests, O Lord God, be clothed with salva-tion, may your saints rejoice in your goodness."

2 Chronicles 6:40-41

❧

Holy Father, there is nothing more important than Your presence in my life. Help me to be a holy place for Your Spirit to dwell. Forgive me of all sin and cleanse my heart of all unrighteousness. Nothing is more comforting to me than to know You are with me, no matter what is happening in my life.

Why We Must Pray for Our Nation

"If my people, who are called by my name, will humble themselves and pray and seek my face and turn from their wicked ways, then will I hear from heaven and will forgive their sin and will heal their land."

2 Chronicles 7:14

❧

Lord God, I come humbly before You and confess the sins of my nation. I pray we as a people would turn from our wicked ways and seek Your face so that You will hear our prayers, forgive our sins, and heal our land. We desperately need Your hand of blessing and protection upon our country. Pour out Your Spirit on us and work Your righteousness in the hearts of the people.

Even When We Don't Do Everything Right

"Although most of the many people who came from Ephraim, Manasseh, Issachar and Zebulun had not purified themselves, yet they ate the Passover, contrary to what was written. But Hezekiah prayed for them, saying, 'May the LORD, who is good, pardon everyone who sets his heart on seeking God—the LORD, the God of his fathers—even if he is not clean according to the rules of the sanctuary.' And the Lord heard Hezekiah and healed the people."

2 Chronicles 30:18-20

❧

God, I thank You that even when I don't do everything right, You see in my heart the desire to do so, and You bless me with answers to my prayers. I am grateful You look past my imperfections and see the perfect qualities of Your Son, Jesus, stamped on my heart instead. Help me to live Your way so that my ways are pleasing in Your sight.

The Power of Fasting with Prayer

"So we fasted and petitioned our God about this, and he answered our prayer."

Ezra 8:23

❧

Lord, help me to fast and pray regularly. Show me how often and how long and give me the strength to get through each fast successfully. With every fast, help me to pray powerfully about the issues of my life and the situations in my world. I want to deny my flesh so that I can exalt You above everything else in my life.

Thank God for His Mercy to You

"But in your great mercy you did not put an end to them or abandon them, for you are a gracious and merciful God."

Nehemiah 9:31

❦

LORD, I am aware every day of Your great mercy toward me. Thank You that You have never judged me according to what I have deserved. Your grace toward me is beyond comprehension. Thank You that You will never forsake me. Help me to never forsake You in any way, either. I pray that my attitude will always be right before You, and I will never take Your mercy for granted.

THE POWER OF ONE

"Go, gather together all the Jews who are in Susa, and fast for me. Do not eat or drink for three days, night or day. I and my maids will fast as you do. When this is done, I will go to the king, even though it is against the law. And if I perish, I perish."

ESTHER 4:16

❧

LORD, I pray You would help me to be a person who has a heart for You and Your ways, and one who is in the right place at the right time. Enable me, as I fast and pray, to have a powerful effect on the world around me by standing up for what is right and following Your leading. Make my prayers powerful enough to save the lives of the people for whom I pray.

Praising God in Good Times and Bad

"At this, Job got up and tore his robe and shaved his head. Then he fell to the ground in worship and said: 'Naked I came from my mother's womb, and naked I will depart. The LORD gave and the LORD has taken away; may the name of the LORD be praised.'"

JOB 1:20-21

❧

DEAR GOD, I will praise You no matter what is happening in my life—in good times and in bad times. Even in the midst of loss, disappointment, sickness, or failure, I lift up praise to You because I know every time I do, You will work powerfully in my situation and be glorified in the process.

Facing Your Fears

"What I feared has come upon me; what I dreaded has happened to me. I have no peace, no quietness; I have no rest, but only turmoil."

Job 3:25-26

❧

Lord, I lift up to You my deepest fears and ask that You would deliver me from them. Set me free from all dread and anxiety about the things that frighten me. Thank You that in Your presence all fear is gone. Thank You that in the midst of Your perfect love, all fear in me is dissolved. You are greater than anything I face.

Knowing God Is with You

"What is man that you make so much of him, that you give him so much attention?"

Job 7:17

❧

Heavenly Father, it is hard to comprehend the depth of Your love for me and why You care about the details of my life. I am grateful that in difficult times You are with me, walking beside me all the way through to the other side of pain and trouble. Where bad things have happened and I have blamed You, I ask for Your forgiveness. Thank You for working things out for my good.

Finding a Song in the Night

"No one says, 'Where is God my Maker, who gives songs in the night?'"

Job 35:10

❧

Lord, Your Word says that when we seek You, You will give us a song in the night. When I am going through a dark night of the soul, I pray You would enlighten my darkness with Your presence. In the face of the darkest situation in my life, I lift up songs of praise to You, knowing Your presence will inhabit them.

Look to God as Your Protector

"'Because of the oppression of the weak and the groaning of the needy, I will now arise,' says the Lord. 'I will protect them from those who malign them.'"

Psalm 12:5

❧

Lord, I am grateful for all the times You have protected me from disaster. I'm sure there are countless ways You have kept me from harm that I am not even aware of. I pray You will always protect me and my reputation from anyone who would try to destroy me. Thank You that You hear my prayers for protection and You have promised to keep me safe.

THE BLESSING OF CONFESSING

"Then I acknowledged my sin to you and did not cover up my iniquity. I said, 'I will confess my transgressions to the LORD'— and you forgave the guilt of my sin."

PSALM 32:5

❧

DEAR LORD, I don't want anything to separate me from You and all You have for me—especially not my own unconfessed sin. I don't want to build a wall between You and me by failing to acknowledge anything I thought, said, or did that was not pleasing in Your sight. If I am too blind to see the truth about myself, reveal it to me so that I can confess it before You.

Pray to Resist Temptation

"Create in me a pure heart, O God, and renew a steadfast spirit within me. Do not cast me from your presence or take your Holy Spirit from me. Restore to me the joy of your salvation and grant me a willing spirit, to sustain me."

Psalm 51:10-12

God, I pray You would create in me a clean and right heart before You at all times. Help me to come to You immediately at the very first sign of temptation so that I can stop any wrong thoughts from turning into sinful actions. I don't want to ever be separated from the presence of Your Holy Spirit.

Thirsting After God

"O God, you are my God, earnestly I seek you; my soul thirsts for you, my body longs for you, in a dry and weary land where there is no water."

Psalm 63:1

❧

Lord God, more than anything else I want Your presence in my life. I long for more of You the way I long for water in the dry heat of summer. I come to You to quench my spiritual thirst as only You can do. Flow Your rivers of living water into me so they can revive my soul and then flow through me to a dry and thirsty world.

Praying from a Right Heart

"If I had cherished sin in my heart, the Lord would not have listened; but God has surely listened and heard my voice in prayer. Praise be to God, who has not rejected my prayer or withheld his love from me!"

Psalm 66:18-20

❧

Lord, I don't want to entertain sin in my heart. I want my heart to be right before You so that You will always hear my prayers. I know I don't do everything perfectly, so I ask that by the power of Your Holy Spirit You will enable me to keep my heart pure and my hands clean. Thank You for loving me and helping me do what is right in Your sight.

Commit Your Work to God

"May the favor of the Lord our God rest upon us; establish the work of our hands for us—yes, establish the work of our hands."

Psalm 90:17

❧

Dear God, I pray You would bless my work and establish it. I commit all of the work I do to You so that it may be used for Your glory. Give me the strength to accomplish what I must do each day, and the wisdom and ability to do it well. Be in charge of every detail of my work so that it will find favor with others and be successful.

Thank God That He Knows and Loves You

"O Lord, you have searched me and you know me. You know when I sit and when I rise; you perceive my thoughts from afar. You discern my going out and my lying down; you are familiar with all my ways."

Psalm 139:1-3

❧

God, I thank You that You know everything about me and You still love me. You know my thoughts and my mistakes, and You still call me Yours. Thank You that You are always with me—teaching and guiding me, comforting and restoring me—and I am never alone. You, Lord, know me better than I know myself. Help me to know You better too.

The Lord Is Near When We Pray

"The Lord is near to all who call on him,
to all who call on him in truth."

Psalm 145:18

❧

Lord, I draw close to You and thank You that You are close to me. I confess the times when I have doubted You were near, because it seemed my prayers went unanswered. Now I know that doubt is contradictory to Your Word. Please help me to pray even more fervently during times of unanswered prayer instead of being concerned that nothing will change.

Acknowledge God in Every Area of Your Life

"Trust in the Lord with all your heart
and lean not on your own understanding;
in all your ways acknowledge him, and
he will make your paths straight."

Proverbs 3:5-6

❧

Heavenly Father, I ask that You would help me to trust You and Your ways and not depend on my own limited understanding of things. Help me to acknowledge You in every area of my life. If I have shut You out of any part of my life, I ask that You would reveal this to me so I can invite You to reign there. Thank You for making my path straight.

God Hears the Prayers of the Righteous

"The Lord detests the sacrifice of the wicked, but the prayer of the upright pleases him."

Proverbs 15:8

❧

Dear God, how grateful I am that You see me as righteous because of my relationship with Jesus. But I know You also want me to choose to live righteously as well. I pray my thoughts, words, and actions will always be pleasing in Your sight so that my prayers will always be pleasing to Your ears. Enable me to always do what's right.

Ten Good Reasons to Ask God for Wisdom

"Buy the truth and do not sell it; get wisdom, discipline and understanding."

Proverbs 23:23

❦

Lord, I pray You would give me wisdom so that I will have a long life of peace, blessing, and happiness. I know with wisdom comes confidence, protection, security, promotion, and guidance. I pray to have the kind of wisdom that saves me from evil and enables me to make right decisions. Along with that, help me to live with understanding, discipline, and truth.

Timing Is Everything

"He has made everything beautiful in its time. He has also set eternity in the hearts of men; yet they cannot fathom what God has done from beginning to end."

Ecclesiastes 3:11

❧

LORD, I know Your timing is not the same as mine. I want all the answers to my prayers right now. But You want me to be patient and wait on You. I lay my concerns before You and leave the outcome in Your hands. Help me to rest in the knowledge that Your timing is perfect, just as everything You do is perfect.

A Stream of Refreshing

"You are a garden fountain, a well of flowing water streaming down from Lebanon."

Song of Songs 4:15

❧

Lord, fill me afresh with Your Spirit today and overflow me with Your healing stream so that when I am with anyone else, they will sense Your presence. Make me to be like a well of refreshing water flowing out to others. I know You see me through Your Son, Jesus. I pray others will see Jesus in me, even if they don't fully understand what it is they are seeing.

Having Peace About Your Future

"You will keep in perfect peace him whose mind is steadfast, because he trusts in you."

Isaiah 26:3

❧

Dear God, the only reason I have peace about the future is because my future is found in You. Even though I don't know the details about what is to come, I know You know everything, and my future is in Your hands. Help me to walk faithfully with You every day—in prayer and in Your Word—so that I can move into the purposes You have for my life.

Knowing Which Way to Go

"Whether you turn to the right or to the left, your ears will hear a voice behind you, saying, 'This is the way; walk in it.'"

Isaiah 30:21

❧

Lord, speak to me about Your will for my life so that I can always walk in it. Your will is a place of safety and protection for me, and I need to know I am headed in the right direction. Help me to hear Your voice speaking to my heart telling me what to do, especially with regard to the decisions I need to make each day of my life.

Praise Is the Purest Form of Prayer

"I provide water in the desert and streams in the wasteland, to give drink to my people, my chosen, the people I formed for myself that they may proclaim my praise."

Isaiah 43:20-21

❧

God, I want to show my love, reverence, devotion, and appreciation for You as I lift You up in worship. I praise You for who You are and for all You have done in this world and in my life. Help me to live every day with praise and thanksgiving in my heart so that I will fulfill my greatest purpose and calling on this earth—which is to worship and glorify You.

Praying God's Word

"As the rain and the snow come down from heaven, and do not return to it without watering the earth and making it bud and flourish...so is my word that goes out from my mouth: It will not return to me empty, but will accomplish what I desire and achieve the purpose for which I sent it."

Isaiah 55:10-11

❧

Heavenly Father, I thank You that Your Word always accomplishes the purpose for which You sent it. Enable me to secure the power and life that is in Your Word by having it planted so firmly in my heart that it guides everything I do. Help me to weave Your Word into my prayers so that it becomes a powerful weapon against which the enemy cannot prevail.

Finding Deliverance

"For Zion's sake I will not keep silent, for Jerusalem's sake I will not remain quiet, till her righteousness shines out like the dawn, her salvation like a blazing torch."

Isaiah 62:1

❧

Lord, I know my only hope for deliverance and restoration in my life is found in You. You have saved me for eternity and for Your glory, and nothing is impossible with You. I pray You will not give up on me until I am completely set free and restored to total wholeness, and my righteousness shines forth like the morning sun.

Praying for Your Nation

"This is what the Lord says: 'Stand at the crossroads and look; ask for the ancient paths, ask where the good way is, and walk in it, and you will find rest for your souls. But you said, "We will not walk in it."...I am bringing disaster on this people, the fruit of their schemes, because they have not listened to my words.'"

Jeremiah 6:16,19

❧

Lord, I come humbly before You and confess the sins of my nation. Even though there are many people who believe in You, far too many have refused to walk Your way. I stand in the gap at the crossroads and look for the good way and pray for many more to join me in walking according to Your law so that disaster will be averted in our land.

Praying for Healing

"Heal me, O Lord, and I will be healed."

Jeremiah 17:14

❧

Dear Lord, how grateful I am that You came as our Healer. Thank You for mercifully understanding how much we need Your healing hand. I ask for Your healing touch upon my body today and whenever I need it. I know when You heal me, I will be healed completely. At the same time I ask for Your guidance and wisdom in knowing how to take care of my body.

Ask God for Discernment

"This is what the Lord Almighty says: 'Do not listen to what the prophets are prophesying to you; they fill you with false hopes. They speak visions from their own minds, not from the mouth of the Lord.'"

Jeremiah 23:16

God, help me to hear Your voice speaking to my heart. Give me discernment so I can always distinguish between those who speak Your truth and those who give false prophesies filled either with fear or false hope. Help me to examine what I hear against the teaching of Your Word. Holy Spirit, guide me in all truth just as You have promised. Help me to identify what is from You and what is not.

God's Plans Still Require Prayer on Our Part

"'I know the plans I have for you,' declares the LORD, *'plans to prosper you and not to harm you, plans to give you hope and a future.'"*

Jeremiah 29:11

❧

LORD, I thank You that Your plans for me are for good—to prosper me and give me a future and a hope. Help me to obey You in every area of my life so that I don't do anything that would thwart Your plans for my future. I seek You about my future now and ask You to help me to hear Your voice leading me every step of the way.

Learning to Listen

"Therefore, this is what the Lord God Almighty, the God of Israel, says: 'Listen!'"

Jeremiah 35:17

❦

Almighty God, help me to be a good listener to Your voice speaking to my heart. I don't want to drown it out with the noise and busyness of life. Help me to take every thought captive in obedience to Your Word. Keep me from entertaining unrighteousness in my thought life. Enable me to be diligent in not allowing anything into my mind that does not glorify You.

Knowing What to Do

"Pray that the Lord your God will tell us where we should go and what we should do."

Jeremiah 42:3

❧

Lord God, I pray You would show me where to go and what to do. I want to always be in the right place at the right time. I lift up to You the specific decisions I need to make today with regard to certain situations in my life. Enable me to hear Your voice instructing me, and help me to do what You are showing me to do.

God Will Get You Through

"Should you then seek great things for yourself? Seek them not. For I will bring disaster on all people, declares the Lord, *but wherever you go I will let you escape with your life."*

Jeremiah 45:5

❧

Lord, I pray You will be with me in the most difficult and trying areas of my life, helping me in ways I may not even be able to comprehend. I know that even though there may be troubles ahead, when I walk with You, You won't let me fall. When I go through difficult situations, I won't complain, for I know You will make a way through or a means of escape.

Finding Hope in the Midst of Sorrow

"Arise, cry out in the night, as the watches of the night begin; pour out your heart like water in the presence of the Lord. Lift up your hands to him."

Lamentations 2:19

❧

Lord, I pour out my heart before You regarding the things in my life that cause me grief. I lift my hands to You because I know You are my hope and Your compassion for me never fails. Heal me of all emotional pain, and use the sorrow I have suffered for good. I pray that in Your presence I will find total restoration.

Finding a New Heart

"I will give them an undivided heart and put a new spirit in them; I will remove from them their heart of stone and give them a heart of flesh."

Ezekiel 11:19

❧

Dear God, I pray You will fill me with Your love, and help me to keep my heart from wandering away from You. Make my heart to be undivided and take away any hard-heartedness in me. I invite You to take charge of my heart and help me to give complete control to You. Light a flame of desire in me for You that never goes out.

Getting Free of the Burden of Sin

"There you will remember your conduct and all the actions by which you have defiled yourselves, and you will loathe yourselves for all the evil you have done."

Ezekiel 20:43

❧

Lord, I don't want to look back over my life—even as recently as yesterday—and feel bad about myself because of the things I have done wrong. Help me to quickly recognize and confess sin. Enable me to live in such a way that I don't have regret over my words, thoughts, or actions. Help me to fully repent so that You will fully lift the burden of sin from me.

Standing in the Gap for Our Nation

"I looked for a man among them who would build up the wall and stand before me in the gap on behalf of the land so I would not have to destroy it, but I found none."

Ezekiel 22:30

❧

Almighty God, I lift up my nation to You, with all its sin and rebellion, and ask that You will have mercy upon us and help us not to reap the full consequences of what we have sown. I stand in the gap to invoke Your power on our behalf. Do not judge us as we deserve, but rather pour out Your Spirit over this land and bring millions of people to You.

Bringing Dead Things to Life

"This is what the Sovereign Lord says to these bones: I will make breath enter you, and you will come to life."

Ezekiel 37:5

Dear God, there are areas of my life that seem dead to me; they need a new infusion of *Your* life. There are dreams I have had that seem as if they have died because for so long they have not yet been realized. I know if You can make dry bones into a vast army, You can bring life to anything worth praying about.

Seeing God in the Dark

"During the night the mystery was revealed to Daniel in a vision. Then Daniel praised the God of heaven and said: 'Praise be to the name of God for ever and ever; wisdom and power are his.'"

Daniel 2:19-20

❧

Lord, it seems that in the middle of the night all problems appear larger. At those times I am reminded that You never sleep, and I can come to You and cling to Your presence. I pray that at those times You will give me the treasures of darkness, stored in secret places, as You have spoken of in Your Word. I pray You will fill my darkness with Your light and give me rest.

Finding God's Forgiveness and Love

"Take words with you and return to the Lord. Say to him: 'Forgive all our sins and receive us graciously, that we may offer the fruit of our lips.'"

Hosea 14:2

❧

Dear God, I recognize how sinful and needy I am. I know I cannot save myself in any way, but You have saved me in every way. That's why I humble myself before You, first of all in confession of my sins. Secondly, I praise You for all You have done for me by extending Your forgiveness, love, and mercy my way. I love You above all else.

It's Never Too Late to Turn to God

"I will repay you for the years the locusts have eaten—the great locust and the young locust, the other locusts and the locust swarm— my great army that I sent among you."

Joel 2:25

❧

Dear God, I thank You that it is never too late to turn to You and see restoration happen. Even though I may feel there has been time wasted in my life when I didn't live fully for You, I pray You would redeem the time and help me to make up for it. Restore anything that has been lost, wasted, or ruined, and I will give You the glory.

Pray for Godly Friends

"Do two walk together unless they have agreed to do so?"

Amos 3:3

❧

Lord, I pray I would always have good godly friends, and that we would influence, encourage, and inspire each other to walk closer to You. I pray for friends who will tell me the truth in love, give me sound counsel, and be a help in times of trouble. Enable me to be that kind of friend too.

Delivering God's Message

"Should I not be concerned about that great city?"

Jonah 4:11

❧

Lord, I know there are people all around me who need to hear Your message of hope and truth—people whom I might not even notice, but whom You love deeply. Reveal them to me so I can pray for them and perhaps speak a good word from You to them. Prepare their hearts to receive from me and most of all from You.

Rising Up out of the Darkness

"Do not gloat over me, my enemy! Though I have fallen, I will rise. Though I sit in darkness, the Lord will be my light."

Micah 7:8

❧

Thank You, Lord, that even if I were to fall off the path You have for me to walk, You will always be there to lift me up and back on it again when I repent of my sins. I thank You that even if I sink into darkness, You will be my light. I praise You as the light of my life and keeper of the flame that burns in my heart for eternity.

Keep Praying No Matter What

"How long, O Lord, must I call for help, but you do not listen? Or cry out to you, 'Violence!' but you do not save?"

Habakkuk 1:2

Lord, help me to have the understanding and faith I need to keep praying and not give up if my prayers are not answered right away. I know Your ways are perfect. Help me to not become discouraged in the time of waiting for Your help, but rather to continue praying until I see Your will done in all the things You put on my heart to pray about.

THANK GOD FOR HIS LOVE

"The LORD your God is with you, he is mighty to save. He will take great delight in you, he will quiet you with his love, he will rejoice over you with singing."

ZEPHANIAH 3:17

❧

LORD, I have great joy in knowing You are always with me and have the power to save me from the plans of the enemy. Help me to remember at all times—even when I go through difficult situations that shake the very foundation of my soul—that my foundation is in You and my security is sustained by Your great love for me.

Don't Neglect Your Walk with God

"'You expected much, but see, it turned out to be little. What you brought home, I blew away. Why?' declares the LORD Almighty. 'Because of my house, which remains a ruin, while each of you is busy with his own house.'"

HAGGAI 1:9

GOD, help me to not be concerned with outward appearances, selfish pursuits, and the condition of my own house, but rather to be concerned with spiritual growth, unselfish service, and the condition of *Your* house. I want to always have my priorities in order so that my walk with You continues to grow closer and deeper.

BY HIS SPIRIT

"He said to me, 'This is the word of the LORD to Zerubbabel: "Not by might nor by power, but by my Spirit," says the LORD Almighty.'"

ZECHARIAH 4:6

❧

ALMIGHTY GOD, I acknowledge I cannot do all You have called me to do, except that Your Spirit enables me to do it. I depend on You to help me get where I need to go. I worship You as the light of my life who illuminates my path and guides my every step. I praise You as the all-powerful God of the universe for whom nothing is too hard.

The Value of Time Alone with God

"After he had dismissed them, he went up on a mountainside by himself to pray. When evening came, he was there alone."

Matthew 14:23

⚜

Dear Lord, help me to find the time I need every day to be alone with You. Escaping all the diversions and busyness seems to be a constant struggle, and I need a greater ability to shut out everything and find solitude with You in prayer. Help me to secure a place of peace and quiet so that I can hear Your voice speaking to my heart.

CREATING A SYMPHONY OF PRAYER

"Again, I tell you that if two of you on earth agree about anything you ask for, it will be done for you by my Father in heaven."

MATTHEW 18:19

LORD, help me to find believers with whom I can agree in prayer on a regular basis. I pray we will be in agreement about the truth of Your Word and the power of Your Holy Spirit. You have said that one can put a thousand to flight and two can put ten thousand to flight. I pray for enough prayer partners to put all of the enemy's forces attacking our lives to flight.

Learning to Believe

"If you believe, you will receive whatever you ask for in prayer."

Matthew 21:22

❧

Dear God, increase my faith to believe for great things. Help me to have faith enough to not pray too small. I know it is not about trusting in faith itself, but trusting in You. It's not about believing in my own ability to believe, but rather it's believing in Your ability and promise to hear and answer. Take away all unbelief in me.

Finding Freedom from What Keeps You Bound

"He replied, 'This kind can come out only by prayer.'"

Mark 9:29

❧

Lord, I see in Your Word that prayer is the key to being set free, and prayer with fasting is even more powerful. I pray You will help me to understand the authority You have given me in prayer to release Your power from heaven in order to see freedom happen in my life and in the lives of those for whom I pray.

THE POWER OF FORGIVENESS

"When you stand praying, if you hold anything against anyone, forgive him, so that your Father in heaven may forgive you your sins."

MARK 11:25

❧

LORD, I pray You would reveal any place in my heart where I have not forgiven someone. I know I have asked this before, but I also know how easy it is to let resentment build up, even though I try not to allow that to happen. I don't want to forfeit the forgiveness You have for me because I have not forgiven someone else.

Why Prayer Works

"I tell you, though he will not get up and give him the bread because he is his friend, yet because of the man's boldness he will get up and give him as much as he needs."

Luke 11:8

❧

Lord, help me to be bold and persistent in prayer. I don't want to be arrogant or presumptuous, as if You owe me anything, but rather to be confident in what Jesus accomplished on the cross that took away Satan's rule and established Your own. Help me to have great faith in You and Your love so that I am confident enough to ask for great things, knowing that You will answer in a great way.

Let Time with God Take the Place of Worrying

"Who of you by worrying can add a single hour to his life?"

Luke 12:25

❧

Dear God, I pray You would help me to stop worrying about things and start spending more time in Your presence. I know the time I waste by worrying is better used to pray and to hear Your voice speaking to my heart. You are my source of strength, hope, love, peace, and rest, and I want to be connected with You and not the things that concern me.

Pray That Your Faith Will Not Fail

"I have prayed for you, Simon, that your faith may not fail. And when you have turned back, strengthen your brothers."

Luke 22:32

❧

Father God, I pray my faith will not fail when I am put to the test. Help me to resist doubt and fear so that my foundation will be built solidly in Christ and therefore will not crumble. Enable me to be a person who strengthens the faith of others because my faith in You is so strong.

Father, I Forgive Them

"Jesus said, 'Father, forgive them, for they do not know what they are doing.' And they divided up his clothes by casting lots."

Luke 23:34

❧

Lord, I pray You would help me to forgive others the way You do. You willingly forgave the unforgivable. I know I can't forgive the unthinkable without You enabling me to do so. Help me to take my focus off whether people deserve to be forgiven or not and instead focus on becoming more like You.

Responding to God's Love

"God so loved the world that he gave his one and only Son, that whoever believes in him shall not perish but have eternal life."

John 3:16

❧

Lord Jesus, it is hard to comprehend love so great as Yours. You laid down Your life for me so that I can live forever with You. I ask You to help me to lay down my life fully for You in serving Your purpose here on earth. My response to Your first loving me is to love You wholeheartedly in return.

Remaining in Him

"If you remain in me and my words remain in you, ask whatever you wish, and it will be given you."

John 15:7

❧

Lord, help me to walk close to You every day and stay constantly in communication with You—both by talking and listening to You speak to my heart. Help me to stay deeply in Your Word, learning more about You and getting to know You better. Help me to increase in the knowledge of Your ways and Your will.

Jesus' Prayer for You

"My prayer is not for them alone. I pray also for those who will believe in me through their message, that all of them may be one, Father, just as you are in me and I am in you."

John 17:20-21

❦

Lord Jesus, just as You prayed for me to be one with You and one with others, I pray You would help me to do just that. Enable me to always be in unity with other believers, no matter what church, race, culture, denomination, city, state, or country they are from. Use this unity I have with You and with others to draw unbelievers to You.

Believing Without Seeing

"Jesus told him, 'Because you have seen me, you have believed; blessed are those who have not seen and yet have believed.'"

John 20:29

LORD, I know You want to bless me in countless ways that require believing without seeing. Help me to have the kind of strong faith I need in order to overcome all doubt. Help me to have faith in Your Word and Your promises, and in Your love, goodness, and power. Help me to trust that You are answering my prayers even when I can't see it.

Praying for Spiritual Leaders and Servants

"They presented these men to the apostles, who prayed and laid their hands on them."

Acts 6:6

❧

God, I ask You to bless all those in full-time ministry. I pray first of all for my pastor, that You would bless him and his family in every way. I pray for all other pastors and staff members at my church to be blessed by You and led by Your Spirit. Keep them all safe and protect them from any attacks of the enemy. Help them to stand strong against every temptation.

Changing the World with Our Prayers

"While they were worshiping the Lord and fasting, the Holy Spirit said, 'Set apart for me Barnabas and Saul for the work to which I have called them.'"

Acts 13:2

LORD, I know my calling and purpose is revealed in prayer. I know it is defined within a church body of believers with whom I can grow. Help me to be in the church body You want me to be in so that I can pray with others in unity and power and be refined by Your Spirit. Enable me to be set apart for the work You have for me to do.

When We Face Decisions and Difficulties

"Paul and Barnabas appointed elders for them in each church and, with prayer and fasting, committed them to the Lord, in whom they had put their trust."

Acts 14:23

❦

Lord God, I know when I fast and pray my prayers gain new power. Help me to do that whenever I have to make important decisions and I must have Your guidance. Help me to have the discipline to fast regularly so that I can be prepared when I have to make quick decisions. Make me ready to handle the great opportunities You have ahead for me.

When Words Don't Come

"In the same way, the Spirit helps us in our weakness. We do not know what we ought to pray for, but the Spirit himself intercedes for us with groans that words cannot express. And he who searches our hearts knows the mind of the Spirit, because the Spirit intercedes for the saints in accordance with God's will."

Romans 8:26-27

❧

Lord, I don't know how to pray about certain things, but *You* do. Holy Spirit, help me in my weakness by interceding *for* me and *through* me. You know the will of the Father and You know what to pray. Guide me and teach me, especially when I have exhausted all words. Help me to communicate my deepest thoughts, feelings, fears, and doubts, so that my prayers are pleasing to God.

Being Faithful in Prayer

"Be joyful in hope, patient in affliction, faithful in prayer."

Romans 12:12

❧

Lord, make me to be a person of powerful prayer. Teach me how to be a prayer warrior who is always faithful to pray. I don't want to be someone who prays sporadically, but rather a person who is so filled with joy and hope that I keep praying and never give up. Help me to have such great faith that I anticipate great things resulting from each prayer.

Overflowing with Joy, Peace, and Hope

"May the God of hope fill you with all joy and peace as you trust in him, so that you may overflow with hope by the power of the Holy Spirit."

Romans 15:13

❧

Dear God, help me to resist the things that would deplete my soul or minimize my strength. Fill me instead with Your hope, peace, and joy, so much so that they overflow from me to others. I praise You for who You are and thank You that as I do, Your Holy Spirit pours new life into me. Fill me afresh with Your Spirit today and take all hopelessness away.

Finding Order and Peace

"God is not a God of disorder but of peace."

1 Corinthians 14:33

❧

Heavenly Father, I know You are a God of order, and order brings peace. Help me to maintain that same order and peace in my life. Give me the wisdom to not allow anything that would disturb that order and peace to influence my life. Help me to fill my mind with Your Word and my soul with Your Spirit so that there is no room for the enemy's propaganda.

When the Failure of Others Tests Our Faith

"Now we pray to God that you will not do anything wrong. Not that people will see that we have stood the test but that you will do what is right even though we may seem to have failed. For we cannot do anything against the truth, but only for the truth. We are glad whenever we are weak but you are strong; and our prayer is for your perfection."

2 Corinthians 13:7-9

❧

Lord God, when I see the failure of any servant of Yours, I pray it will not shake my faith in the least. Help me to do the right thing and remain strong in You no matter what I see anyone else doing. Give me faith that is not dependent on the rise or fall of others. I know You won't fail, even though others do, and that is all that matters.

Moving Into the Freedom God Has for Us

"It is for freedom that Christ has set us free. Stand firm, then, and do not let yourselves be burdened again by a yoke of slavery."

Galatians 5:1

❧

Lord, help me to stand firm in the freedom You have secured for me. Thank You, Jesus, that You gave Your life so that I could be set free from the yoke of slavery to the enemy of my soul. Help me to not become entangled in it again. Make me aware when I am accepting some bondage in my life for which You died to set me free.

Seeing the Power of God at Work

"I pray also that the eyes of your heart may be enlightened in order that you may know the hope to which he has called you, the riches of his glorious inheritance in the saints, and his incomparably great power for us who believe."

Ephesians 1:18-19

Dear God, I pray the eyes of my heart will be opened to see the hope to which You have called me. Help me to understand my true glorious inheritance. Enable me to comprehend the magnitude of Your power on my behalf because I believe in You. I seek more of Your presence and Your power and I long to see them manifested in my life.

Getting Armed for the Battle

"Put on the full armor of God so that you can take your stand against the devil's schemes...Pray in the Spirit on all occasions with all kinds of prayers and requests. With this in mind, be alert and always keep on praying for all the saints."

Ephesians 6:11,18

LORD, because I have aligned myself with You, the enemy wages war against me. Help me to put on the full spiritual armor You have provided for me. Teach me what that is so I comprehend how to maintain it. Help me to fully understand the depth of truth, righteousness, faith, a solid walk with Christ, salvation, powerful prayer, and the knowledge of Your Word that I need.

Prayer and Thanksgiving Bring Peace

"Do not be anxious about anything, but in everything, by prayer and petition, with thanksgiving, present your requests to God. And the peace of God, which transcends all understanding, will guard your hearts and your minds in Christ Jesus."

Philippians 4:6-7

❧

Dear God, help me to not be anxious or worried about anything. Help me to pray and intercede instead. Enable me to lift up praise and worship in the face of whatever opposes me. Help me to bring every concern before You and leave it at Your feet. Help me to refuse to think what-if thoughts. Fill me with Your peace that passes all understanding so that my heart and mind will be protected.

The Power of Praying for Others

"For this reason, since the day we heard about you, we have not stopped praying for you and asking God to fill you with the knowledge of his will through all spiritual wisdom and understanding."

Colossians 1:9

❧

Lord, I pray for the people You have put in my life and on my heart. Fill them with wisdom and understanding and the knowledge of Your will so that they will stay on the path You have for them. I pray they will learn to hear Your voice and come to know You better, so that they can have a closer walk with You.

How to Always Do God's Will

"Be joyful always; pray continually; give thanks in all circumstances, for this is God's will for you in Christ Jesus."

1 Thessalonians 5:16-18

❦

God, I know it is always Your will for me to be joyful and pray often and give thanks to You in all circumstances. Help me to remember to do Your will in this regard, even when I don't see answers to my prayers as I would like. No matter what is happening in my life, I know You are greater than anything I face.

Praying for People Who Need Good News

"Finally, brothers, pray for us that the message of the Lord may spread rapidly and be honored, just as it was with you."

2 Thessalonians 3:1

❧

Lord, use me to bring the good news of salvation through Jesus Christ to others. Just as You have used others powerfully in my life, equip me with the right words at the right time so that those whose hearts are ready will be drawn toward You. I also pray for the men and women who need the good news, that their hearts would be open to receive all You have for them.

Praying Together in Unity

"I want men everywhere to lift up holy hands in prayer, without anger or disputing."

1 Timothy 2:8

❧

Lord, help me to find other believers who will stand with me in prayer. Bring godly prayer partners into my life with whom I can pray in power. Help us to be so devoted to You that we maintain a oneness of the Spirit, even if we disagree on certain things. I pray we will be unified in our belief in Your Word so that we will be unified in our prayers.

Being Remembered in Prayer

"I thank God, whom I serve, as my forefathers did, with a clear conscience, as night and day I constantly remember you in my prayers."

2 Timothy 1:3

❧

Lord, help me to not forget anyone in my prayers. Especially show me the people who feel forgotten so that I can remember them in intercession. Bring specific people to mind who need a miracle of healing or help. Show me who needs to hear Your voice guiding them. Enable the people I pray for to sense Your love in their lives.

Ask for Boldness to Share Your Faith

"I pray that you may be active in sharing your faith, so that you will have a full understanding of every good thing we have in Christ."

Philemon 1:6

God, help me to get over any inhibitions I have about sharing my faith with unbelievers. I know of no greater gift than to give someone Your love and the good news of salvation in Christ, but I always want to be sensitive to Your leading so that I don't come off as insensitive to others. Help me to have a perfect sense of timing and the right words to say.

Approach God's Throne with Confidence

"We do not have a high priest who is unable to sympathize with our weaknesses, but we have one who has been tempted in every way, just as we are—yet was without sin. Let us then approach the throne of grace with confidence, so that we may receive mercy and find grace to help us in our time of need."

Hebrews 4:15-16

❧

Thank You, Jesus, that You understand my weaknesses and my temptations, for You have been tempted in every way and yet did not sin. Because You understand my struggles, I know I can come to You and receive mercy. Help me to approach You with confidence, knowing You will strengthen me in my time of need.

Asking God for Wisdom

"If any of you lacks wisdom, he should ask God, who gives generously to all without finding fault, and it will be given to him."

James 1:5

❧

God, I ask for wisdom, for I know true wisdom comes only from You. Thank You that Your Word promises You will give wisdom to me when I ask for it. Help me to be wise every day in every decision, especially when I must act quickly. Help me to know what to do and what not to do in any situation.

Powerful and Effective Praying

"Confess your sins to each other and pray for each other so that you may be healed. The prayer of a righteous man is powerful and effective."

James 5:16

❧

Lord, how grateful I am that my righteousness comes not because I do everything perfectly, but because *You* have done everything perfectly. I am seen as righteous because of Your great sacrifice on the cross. Help me to confess my sins not only to You, but also to others who may be affected so that healing can come to us all. Thank You for making my prayers powerful and effective.

God Hears Our Prayers and Sees Our Heart

"The eyes of the Lord are on the righteous and his ears are attentive to their prayer, but the face of the Lord is against those who do evil."

1 Peter 3:12

❦

Dear God, I thank You that You see my heart and hear my prayers. How grateful I am that when You see me, You see the righteousness of Jesus *in* me and not the sinner I was before I received Him into my life. Thank You that You not only hear my prayers, but You see my need and will answer the cries of my heart.

Coming to Father God in Confidence

"This is the confidence we have in approaching God: that if we ask anything according to his will, he hears us. And if we know that he hears us—whatever we ask—we know that we have what we asked of him."

1 John 5:14-15

❧

Heavenly Father, it gives me great confidence to know that if I ask according to Your will, You will hear me and I will have what I ask for. I come to You as Your beloved child and ask You to help me pray according to Your will. I know I will receive only good things from You because You love and accept me.